For Samantha!,

Elaine Flowers

May 21, 2011

I Wouldn't Mind

Having a Husband,

I Just Don't Want To Be Somebody's Wife

The Single Woman's Guide to Self-fulfillment

Published by:
Top Shelf Publishing
Dallas, Texas

Published and printed in the United States of America
Copyright © 2009 Elaine Garcia

First Edition
E-Book (Online Download only)

ISBN - 10: 0-9747388-0-8

Elaine Flowers is not a licensed therapist. Any advice,
suggestions, or counsel given is purely the opinion of the
author and based on her own personal experiences derived
from interactions and a basic studying of people.

All examples given in the book are true accounts but names
have been changed to protect the privacy of people or persons
used to make points.

This book is dedicated to the memory of

a dear friend

and client,

Vikky Lynn Webb Overstreet

A special thank you to the single, married, and divorced women who participated in a survey which assisted me with the writing of this book.

Additional thanks, and my deepest gratitude goes to; EBM Professional Services, and Ray Hodges Event Photography.

Table Of Contents:

Preface

To clear up any misconceptions that the title of this book may suggest let me preface my advice by saying what this book IS NOT about.

This is not a male-bashing book.

This is not an anti-marriage book.

This book is not
promoting any alternative lifestyles where
sexual orientations are concerned.

This book is not promoting adultery.

What you CAN look forward to getting is a clearer understanding on the desire to be married and the need to be in relationships involving the opposite sex.

-

Introduction

This book came out of a necessity that I felt my single-never-been-married women were crying out for. So many idealize marriage, I'm sure in the same way I did before I was married. For me, at a young age, the bubble burst, but women continue to hold on to the fairytale they've had for years.

I was a hairstylist for more than 20 years and had both mature and younger clients who over the years expressed their wishes on finding a husband and being married or even just finding that special someone. This seemed to be a constant topic of conversation with said women. I must add that many of my married clients often said "If something ever happens to my husband, I don't think I'll ever get married again." They didn't regret, necessarily getting married but they wouldn't rush to do it again.

Love and marriage do not necessarily coincide, but people assume they do. Understandably, it's a logical assumption—you fall in love, you get married and live happily ever after. If only life were so simple.

Not only did many of my clients talk to me about men and relationships, they came to me eager to unload or sometimes get advice—the hairstyle was just a bonus treat. At the time I didn't see these appointment times as counseling sessions but many of them were.

There was once an occasion when a client, Merylon sat in my chair and after I asked her how she wanted her hair styled, she burst into tears. This was early in my profession, not to mention I was young with little life experience. I asked her was she okay, not knowing really what else to say or do. She told me she had been diagnosed with cancer the day before.

Of course, I was at a loss for how to handle the situation. All I wanted was to begin shampooing her so I could get to the next client who would soon be coming. I fail to remember what I said to her. I do remember how bad I felt and how I didn't really know an adequate way to express it. To make a short story shorter, her health faded fairly quickly and because of the discomfort I felt I never went to visit her as her health declined nor did I attend her funeral. I felt horrible and ashamed about the way I handled that for years. *I didn't even attend her funeral.*

Since then, I've matured I know she understands my immaturity at the time and even forgives me if my actions offended her in any way. It took me a while to get there, but I did get there. And one of the things I came to learn is when clients come in, sometime it is just about the hairstyle but sometimes it's about more. The hydraulic chair has strange effects on clients and can be likened to that of a therapist's couch. It's the feel of relaxation that causes them to let go and unload, or the increased trust factor—they trust you with their most prized possession (their hair) so they trust you with everything else. Maybe it's both of those things.

Over time, I've listened to women's problems, made suggestions, given advice—sometimes good and sometimes bad—made friends and enemies. I've learned so much and probably forgotten just as much but I do know that everyone wants to be heard, seen and identified with. *We all want to be validated.*

So, here's to you, single ladies!

I Wouldn't Mind Having A Husband, I Just Don't Want To Be Somebody's Wife, designed for readers who want to skip the jargon, and get to the point quickly. This book will also help you to put down the rose colored glasses, and bravely, as well as eagerly take a good look at life so that you are ready to embrace a promising future saturated with love and fulfillment.

There will be some advice in this book you may not expect, agree with at first (or ever), or may be startling. Paramount to any other motivation, I hope that the information you will uncover here will make you think even if you do not agree. Also, understand that there is no *one* answer for every woman. With that said—

Prepare yourself to laugh and think!

Section 1

Marriage Is a Calling

I, for one, being divorced for nearly a score of years, have come to the conclusion that not only would I not make a good girlfriend, I would also make a horrible wife—in the traditional sense. I have totally made peace with this and with such realization it has helped me to look into the plight of so many single women who believe they want to marry and are earnestly hoping to be scooped up by Mr. Right, or his half brother, Prince Charming, and carried off into the sunset.

I have heard so many single women say how much they want to be married that it makes me want to just scream. It doesn't upset me that women want to be married it's just that I know most of them have no clue as to what it is they're wishing for. And, I believe if they new what I, and many married women knew, they would thank God everyday, and bask in the beauty of their singleness.

Years ago I assumed, like a lot of women do, that marriage was what I wanted. Most women see marriage as a natural progression, or one of the many steps you take in life. You're born, grow up, fall in love, get married, have children and die. You may interject other things like education and career but basically we expected our lives to go something like this. I too adopted these same systematic rules from society.

Marriage is a ministry and you must be called to it for it to be successful. God calls those who are made for the ministry of marriage and He joins those He calls for that work. There are so many miserable, married people because *they* have joined *themselves* with another person without the consent of God.

When people marry who are not called for the position it becomes a bad representation of what marriage is or should be about. I was one of those people. I wasn't called for marriage at the time I married, and like so many other unions, it was disastrous.

Those of you who are dating, or considering marriage should imagine a series of worse case scenarios involving your partner. Not in a morbid sense, but in a realistic way.

Minding the fact you two haven't had the luxury of thirty or forty years of wedded bliss, and you are afforded the

> When people marry who are not called for the position it becomes a bad representation of what marriage is or should be about.

insight into the future and could see that the day after your wedding, one of you is in a debilitating accident where the other will have to provide around the clock care for the injured spouse for many years to come and possibly for the rest of your lives together. Would either of you still go through with the marriage? Before being faced with taking care of a spouse, answer these questions.

Do you trust the fact that the other person loves you enough to take on the responsibility?

What would either of your attitudes be like if put in the predicament of taking on the position of caregiver for the other?

Do you love your potential spouse enough to go ahead with the marriage knowing you will be taking care of him in a possibly vegetative state for an undetermined amount of time?

Think the questions over. There are no right or wrong answers; just know what to do after you come up with the answer.

Or how about this—a month after you marry Prince Charming he has some devastating financial woes where you both lose everything. His father, King Charming is dethroned and the two of you have to move out of the castle and into a homeless shelter for an undetermined amount of time. If you could see into the future and knew this in advance:

Would you still take the plunge?

What would your response, or behavior be after it happened?

Say you go through with the marriage:
Would you be a "ride or die" chick and follow him to a shelter, or under a bridge. Perhaps, would you say "Bump that" and go home to your family and leave him to figure it out?

Getting married when you aren't called is the same as thinking just because you have exceptional oratorical skills you should become a preacher. Neither of these proves to be very affective. The important thing is to recognize, through prayer and God's revelation, if you're called or not.

Ken & Barbie

Standing behind a hydraulic chair beautifying women you learn a lot. One client in particular who had met her husband in college sat down one day and unloaded her grief. The couple, who looked like the living version of the black Ken and Barbie dolls, also appeared to be an ideal couple. Of course, not necessarily being negative, I never believe in the fairytale like so many others but even I thought that they were a exceptional couple.

> "*Whenever I saw our other married friends having problems and getting divorces I would always say it's too bad that everyone doesn't have what we have.*"

This client, let's call her Barbie, began telling me of the shattering of her world when she discovered that Ken had cheated on her. But it wasn't as simple as once or twice, it was multiple, anonymous encounters with women, even involving pornography on some level. Her world as she knew it was over and the incredulity of it all left her totally devastated. Her utter disbelief led me to ask her *'Who did you believe you and your husband to be before this happened?'*

Barbie understood my question perfectly and after pondering it for a moment her response was *"Whenever I saw our other married friends having problems and getting divorces I would always say it's too bad that they don't have what we have."* Even she believed that they had something rare and uncommon. And the truth is if they find a way past these issues in particular they will have a marriage that is rare and uncommon.

I didn't understand how she could live with Ken all of those years and not know who he was or what he was capable of. But it happens everyday in a lot of marriages. Of course I don't blame her for what he did but living with blinders on is setting yourself up to be blindsided.

What are your ideas about marriage and relationships in general? What are your ideas about the way people treat each other? How were you raised? What did you see growing up? What are your ideas about people doing bad things to each other,

> *One area where women mess up is when they have these storybook illusions of how they see their lives playing out and of how they view the significant man in their lives.*

intentional or unintentional? How different do you believe your relationship to be than that of your parents? What are your true views on forgiveness?

Being a realist I'm sometimes accused of being negative or pessimistic. But I have learned the value of being true to myself regardless. When Prince Charming walks in and approaches me I am waiting for the other shoe to fall. Some may see this as negative but I can't truly appreciate a person or let myself go until I'm sitting with the *real* person.

When I was about four or five years old my sister who is five years my senior was explaining to me how Santa Clause was going to go all around the world in one night and take toys to every little boy and girl. Before she told me that story, I sort of halfway believed in Santa not knowing exactly how it was all supposed to work, but after she let me in on the details I knew the whole thing was ridiculous. I never fell for it, ever. And to make matters worse, I think *she* really believed what she was telling me. I knew then, that I was different from the average child.

Being true to oneself can be viewed as illiberal in a way. When you don't buy into what others consider *the norm* they don't' get it. Neither do they understand when you don't buy into society falsehoods or go along to get along. Being true to you, takes courage.

With counseling, Ken and Barbie found their way back, but believe me, the weighted sacrifices were on Barbie's side of the scale.

Illusions and delusions

One area where women mess up is when they have these storybook illusions of how they see their lives playing out and of how they view the significant man in their lives. The moment he does something outside of the idea that she has in her head, the fairytale is over, and she is devastated and can't imagine how things could've gone so wrong.

The way to fix this is to let go of the storybook fantasies. Don't idealize marriage and think it's the answer to all of your problems. When you really take the time to assess why you want to be married does it go a little something like this?

1. It would be nice to have someone paying (or helping to pay) my bills.
2. It would be nice to have sex on the regular without guilt.
3. It would be nice to have some constant companionship.
4. I want to escape this life I'm currently living.

Let us address each of these individually.

1.) *It would be nice to have someone paying (or helping to pay) my bills.*

It's true that a husband is supposed to provide and protect, but if this is your reason for wanting a husband you are in for a rude awakening. Having a husband isn't like winning the lottery and you are now going to be on a life-long shopping spree. It means you now have someone to answer to about all financial decisions.

And let's say you marry someone with poor spending habits, or spending habits different from yours. In this case you will be on a life-long struggle of trying to make ends meet or come to a meeting of the minds. Marrying someone for money or financial security is unfulfilling, wrong and a poor representation of marriage and what God had in mind when he created it. Proverbs 31:17-18 not only speaks to the wife's contribution to a marriage, the virtuous woman's daily workload is extensive and certainly more so than any single woman's.

2.) *It would be nice to have sex on the regular without guilt.*

Okay, this is a tricky one and should be looked at from a few different angles. You know the cliché about air not being that important until your not getting any? Well, sex is kind of like that. It's not that big a deal until you're going without but then the flip side is, it's only good when you're not under any obligation to do it.

As a married woman your body belongs to your husband and vice-versa. When two people are sexually compatible there should be minimal problems but if they're not, somebody is feeling used while the other is feeling cheated. Having sex on a regular basis should never be a reason to get married because sex alone cannot sustain the union.

3.) *It would be nice to have some constant companionship.*

A marriage based on companionship alone is something that may be acceptable when you're talking about senior citizens hooking up to keep each other company. But when you're talking about young adults who get together because they're tired of being alone is a disaster waiting to happen.

Marriage is never a cure for loneliness. In fact, the loneliest time of my life was when I was married. Having someone around who doesn't get you and you don't really get them is frustrating, to say the least.

Being divorced for quite some time, I have gone back and forth over thinking that I want to marry again. It's been a long time but I used to think I wanted to give it another try and then I thought about it and it dawned on me that my reasons for wanting to do it had nothing to do with the ministry of marriage at all. It was all for my own self-serving reasons, which without a doubt would've landed me right back into what I had gotten out of.

You can have a full life with family, loved ones and, both male and female friends with out getting married. Believe it or not these other options can be very fulfilling.

4) *I want to escape this life I'm currently living.*

Until you are complete and whole within yourself you are no good for a partnership. And believing that an escape into another life is going to get you away from your problems is unrealistic. Whatever your issues are now will most certainly still be your issues, when your location and status changes.

After graduating high school I enrolled in cosmetology school after the thwarted plans to take the beauty industry in California by storm. I came home and discovered that all of my friends were away at college and doing other interesting things so I felt I needed to do more.

Enters scene: a man to help me escape my humdrum life. Not just a man, but one who looked good on paper. He came from a respectable family and had already settled into a career.

And to prove to you it wasn't just me looking for an escape, my proposal for marriage from him went something like this; "I'm tired of saying girlfriend, I'm ready to call somebody my wife." We hadn't been together long so he couldn't have been tired of calling me girlfriend. He had been in a relationship for several years prior to meeting me and suffered a bad break up. He was looking to escape his problems and I was the perfect victim.

Although he was older, we were both still living at home with our parents at the time. It is so obvious now we were using each other to start new lives. In essence, our motivations about entering into a covenant of, *until death do we part,* were misunderstood and misguided. Especially when you measure in immaturity on both our parts.

There is nothing wrong with wanting relationships in fact God made us for relationships according to Romans 12:10 *Be kindly affectioned one to another with brotherly love; in honour preferring one another.* I think what happens is when we see married couples we envy, or idealize what we think they have with each other. But the sad truth is, we may not be equipped for marriage lifestyle.

Why aren't you married?

To all of my single sisters over, let's say 30 years of age, how many times have you had someone ask you why you haven't married or when are you going to settle down and get married? What's worse than that is when they don't ask you anything but they give you the look of pity if the subject comes up as if to say, "Poor you. You can't find yourself a man to marry." Then they think of all the reasons why you probably don't have a man who wants to marry you.

So you're either left feeling defensive and ready to explain that you have failed to find whatever good men still out there or the pressure is on for you to find Mr. Wonderful. Probably the real reason you haven't gotten married is because God is trying to save you from a life of misery. He knows you are not ready or it's not His plan for your life so He is sparing you the grief.

Because of pressure from others some women get so desperate to get married that the first man who comes along that looks like a decent candidate, they throw caution to the wind and figure even if it doesn't work out at least they can say they've done it once. For some, being divorced is better than saying they have never been married at all.

Based on statistics, with there being eight women to one man (and this gap is widening every day) there are a whole lot of women who will never experience wedded bliss—or wedded misery. But never fear; if being married is your calling and it is your desire to walk in God's purpose then there is a man especially designed in perfect divinity for you. All you have to do is ask God and then listen for His answer.

Having the right ideas about marriage is extremely important if you are considering it. When I speak of "ideas" what I'm referring to is; do you love the person you're involved with or do you love the idea of them and what they represent?

If the circumstances surrounding your relationship changes do your feelings remain the same for the person or is that the end of your love? All I'm saying is be honest with yourself about the intentions you have regarding marriage, and be mature when seeking the truth of the basis of your relationship.

In *The Purpose Driven Life*[1] by Rick Warren, he speaks of driving forces, which shapes each of our lives. The list goes as; many people are driven by

- Guilt
- Resentment and anger
- Fear
- Need for approval

Do you feel guilty because you are tempted or you are having unmarried sex?

Are you resentful or angry about the fact that someone you have been involved with hasn't married you? Do you fear that time is running out or that there is something wrong with you because you haven't married yet? Does your need for approval drive you to want to be married?

Section End:
Questions to ponder and to motivate introspection.

1. Do you feel lacking or uncomfortable in a room with nothing but couples?
2. Do you believe most married couples have the ideal life?
3. Do you honestly know what characteristics make a good wife?
4. Do you have what it takes to make a good wife?
5. Do you know what characteristics make a good husband?
6. Do you believe marriage to be the answer to all of your problems?
7. Do you believe that God has called you to the ministry of marriage?

There are no right or wrong answers, but consider them and why you may feel the way that you do. Do your best to find your own personal truth.

Section 2

What Are Your Examples Of Marriage?

Funny, but not necessarily true:

Three men are sitting around boasting about how they had enforced household duties on their new wives.

The first man, who'd married an Asian woman laughed and said that he had told his wife she was going to do all the dishes, the laundry and the house cleaning. He said, it took a few days before she caught on and when the third day arrived he came home to a clean house and the laundry, and dishes were done.

The second man, who'd married a white woman teased that he had given his wife orders. She alone was to do all the cleaning, dishes and the cooking. On the first day he didn't see any results, but the next day it was better. By the third day she'd conformed and his house was clean, the dishes were done and there was a huge dinner on the table waiting for him.

The third man's wife was a black woman. Loudly and boastfully, he said he had told her that her duties were to keep his house clean, wash his dishes, mow his lawn, do his laundry, and have hot food on the table for every single meal.

He said the first day he didn't' see anything, the second day he didn't see anything but by the third day most of the swelling had gone down and he could see a little out of his left eye; enough to fix himself a bite to eat, load the washing machine and call a landscaper.

I don't want to add to the stereotype of the angry, combative black woman, especially since women of any race can fall victim to physical abuse, but I couldn't resist.

> *Never seeing what the role of husband looked like made me ill equipped for marriage.*

Realistically, a lot of men, instead of hiring a maid, a cook and or a personal assistant, will decide to marry and expect — or demand a woman to take on those responsibilities. Being his wife is full of duties he expects his woman to take on and there is nothing romantic whatsoever about that.

There are women who basically do the same thing. They marry men thinking that having him around is necessary for all the things they don't want to handle like working, car maintenance and handling finances.

This can be attributed to the examples of marriage these women had while growing up. And when they don't have an example, as in my case, it's even more difficult. Being raised by a single mother with a strong, dominant personality my example of a husband's role was non-existent.

Even during the time period when there was a stepfather present in our home while I was growing up my mother was still 'head of household', if you will, and the all-in-all decision maker.

I remember thinking during the looong five years of my marriage that my husband was in the way. This was simply because I didn't understand a husbands role and therefore didn't really understand my own role as wife. Never seeing what the role of husband looked like made me ill equipped for marriage. This is a problem for a lot of women not just because of the lacking father figure but because of the domineering women they've had as examples.

I don't profess to have all of the answers since I haven't successfully played the part of wife myself. But some things are simply common sense.

There are many examples of marriage. There are also certain types of spouses that should be avoided at all cost, such as;

- Judgmental Spouse
- Controlling Spouse
- Nagging Spouse
- Emotionally Unavailable Spouse
- Possessive Spouse
- Abusive Spouse

When you witness a couple where one of the partners is very critical of the other you think that you would never let yourself get caught in a situation like that. But, it's easier to do than you might think. In a new relationship, criticism may take on the appearance of the other person assisting you with self-improvement and can seem perfectly innocent in the beginning. Someone who is constantly critical of the person they're supposed to love most will ruin true intimacy. This is true in platonic friendships as well.

When this happens a person is compelled to live a life outside of the relationship because they don't feel free to be themselves.

Truth, honesty and the freedom to be yourself are the keys to real intimacy. When a person feels safe to show their true selves and is without fear of ridicule it is the beginning to a real relationship with another person.

Judgmental spouse. I used to have this client who came to me for a hair weave. One day she called to discuss her hair and her husband walked into the room so she began speaking in code. When she finally came in for her appointment I asked her about it and she told me that her husband didn't know her hair wasn't all hers. I couldn't believe it. I asked her why she didn't feel like she could tell him about the extensions. (As far as I'm concerned, wigs and hair weave, in this day in time, are no more than accessories like earrings and bracelets). She responded that years before, before they were even married, he discovered a weft of hair in her things and with a look of total disgust, told her she'd better not ever put it in her hair.

I couldn't leave it alone, so I then asked her hadn't he ever run his fingers through her hair and felt the tracks? She said that whenever he touched her hair she would just duck and move out of the way, asking him not to mess up her style.

Being in, what's supposed to be an intimate relationship but feeling the need to hide something so (to me) inconsequential as that was so sad. Not only sad, but also exhausting. All of the lying, sneaking and deception that had to go into play. It made me sad for them because the people at home should be the ones you can be yourself around if no one else.

The first time you are tempted to hide your real self from your man is a sure sign you don't trust him, and after you move forward with the untruth you have turned into someone he can't trust. And believe me it snowballs from there and the lies and falsehoods only get bigger and more intense.

You turn into someone he doesn't recognize and chances are he's hiding things from you that he believes you can't handle. Sooner rather than later you both become resentful of each other and the relation-ship as well as the time you've wasted living a lie. This is the kind of thing that should've been dealt with immediately. Instead of her responding with fear (of whatever) and conceding to his request of not using the original weft of hair she should have countered with a challenge of her own like, "And if I do add this hair into my own what's gonna happen?" Or, "Honey, even your mother wears a wig so why would it be a problem if I wear a weave?" Once you let something like this go unresolved it is so difficult to recover from.

Controlling Spouse. Another former client of mine had a husband she'd married while he was incarcerated. Of course, in the beginning he was very attentive (or as attentive as he could be seeing as he was locked up) as well as loving and supportive. While he was away she had built a successful life for herself professionally and became very active in her church. Once he was released and was placed in a halfway house he began dictating her comings and goings.

> The first time you are tempted to hide your real self from your man is a sure sign you don't trust him, and after you move forward with the untruth you have turned into someone he can't trust.

When he finally came home to her, he watched her every move. He worked a second-shift plant job and on his lunch breaks around eight o'clock in the evening he demanded (you heard me)she come to the caféteria where he worked and have dinner with him. She didn't have a choice. He wanted to know her exact whereabouts every minute of the day. He checked the gas and mileage on her car and phone records to see whom she had been interacting with. This man had been released from prison, and built one for her.

When he displayed this conduct before getting out she assigned it to his frustration of being behind bars along with his deep love and affection for her. She made the grave error of overlooking his abhorrent behavior and suffered great consequences.

A partner who is **nagging, emotionally unavailable, possessive** or **abusive** all display signs in the beginning. A nagger is someone who is usually hard to satisfy and is very needy. Those who are emotionally unavailable almost always have some inner turmoil going on, such as an addiction of some sort.

A **possessive spouse** has abandonment issues or separation anxiety usually deriving from a childhood experience or an earlier volatile relationship, which ended badly. This is why it is so important to spend the time it takes to get to know a person and their family. So many times women don't take this time because they're afraid of what they'll find thus ruining their dream of getting married. Some women don't believe they can have what they really want in a relationship; in fact most people don't believe this so they settle. These relationships or marriages usually progress very quickly, which is how the women find themselves trapped in a nightmare.

An **Abusive Spouse** displays a lot of the same characteristics as the controlling spouse. And many times those two go hand in hand. There are always signs, such as uncontrollable anger; inappropriate anger and a history of abuse. Therefore, another reason women should take the time needed to get to know a potential spouse.

Who Were You?

After a break up between two people, those closest to them hear all of the negative things about the other person and how could that person have done them so wrong. What we never hear—or say, if we are that person—is our own responsibility.

So, who were *you* that you chose such a person? When you mate called you low down dirty names, who were you that you continued on? Who were you in the first place that you attracted such a person? Who were you when you chose a person who was addicted to drugs or alcohol? Who were you when you chose a person who habitually cheated on you? Who were you that you overlooked a person physically or mentally abusing you.

Addressing this issue is more important than any other when you are healing from such hurts. Looking inward instead of at the other person is the smartest way to deal with such situations. We can't fix another person, and further, it's not our responsibility. This should be left to the professionals. But, what we can do is use this opportunity for introspection and growth. And doing this by understanding ourselves and our own involvement in the relationship.

I, like many people was upset with Chris Brown during the ordeal with he and Rihana. I was upset with her too but not as much, until she went back to him. What is easy to recognize in couples like them is that the two of them, not just one, are unhealthy. It's not just one or the other. They both have a sickness that draws them together.

So, the question remains; who are you when you enter unhealthy relationships?

Love and happiness

It's been said, to be happy with a man, a woman must understand him a lot and love him a little. But, in order to be happy with a woman, a man must love her a lot and never try to understand her at all.

One of the biggest problems between men and women is that neither group appreciates the differences of the other group. Men are goal-oriented and focus on the outcome and women are process-oriented and are more concerned with the procedure, which leads to the outcome.

A traditional man would never want a woman who displayed too many masculine characteristics and a traditional woman would never want a man who displayed too many feminine characteristics. Gary Smalley in *For Better Or For Best: Understand Your Man*, says "Your husband can become more sensitive through indirect methods, rather than through direct confrontation[1]. *Sensitive?* We often hear women say they want a sensitive man. Do we? No. What we really want is a man who can appreciate *our* sensitivity. I know that's what I would want!

I suffer from arachnophobia (fear of spiders) and ornithophobia (fear of birds). Back in the day I had such an intense fear that I developed a keen sixth sense of knowing when a spider had entered the room. And I have many upon many frightening (to me) spider and bird stories, including a bird getting inside the house. Yikes! Not only do I run from birds or make loud noises to get them to fly away, I also have many cans of Raid (in the red can—works instantaneously) stationed all around the house (and in the car) for easy access in the event that a spider shows up.

Years ago, I was enjoying the company of a guy I was dating at the time while watching movies one evening. Sitting on the sofa, we both spotted a spider at the same time crawling on an adjacent wall. And lo and behold if he didn't jump up, scurrying around for one of my many cans of Raid I kept. He found the can, and standing three feet away with his arm stretched out as far as it would go, began drowning the spider in Raid foam until it was chemically fried to death. And you know what happened. There, shortly after that incident was the end of said love affair.

I just couldn't do it. We cannot BOTH be afraid of spiders! Him being afraid of spiders was just too girlie for my taste. Men are supposed to be hunters and women gatherers. What kind of hunter is afraid of spiders?

> *If I'm getting my nails done, and he's getting his nails done— Who's gonna change the flat?*

I feel the same way about men getting their nails done. If I'm getting my nails done, and he's getting his nails done—*Who's gonna change the flat?* There isn't anything wrong with a little sexism. Roles should be clearly defined, but unfortunately the gender gap seems to be closing. The world is slowly (or quickly) moving to an erogenous zone that is certainly uncomfortable.

Seriously, maybe it is okay for a man to be afraid of insects and it may not be a big deal for a man to get a manicure but there is a need for balance. I believe that if a man's blood pressure rises every time he sees eight hairy legs crawling in his direction he should hook up with a woman who was raised in the wilderness.

In a marriage, there really is only room for one damsel, one scary person and one pretty person. If you don't believe me ask Halle and Eric.

Necessity and Needs

During the Christmas season some years back, a client of mine who, like clockwork, came in every Wednesday at four o'clock without fail. Charla, I'll call her, a beautiful, middle-aged woman with a lovely personality to go along with her looks, sat down in my chair and I could hardly wait to tell her I'd ran into her husband at the mall as he was shopping for her Christmas gift. She and I were close in this way, for we had known each other for many years. After all, this was husband number three for her and I really thought they made a great couple and that he was "the one."

When I saw Tony in the mall, in his bewilderment, he told me he was struggling on what to get Charla because she had pretty much everything already. She was a woman who wore lots of nice jewelry, cared a lot about her appearance and had lots of nice things in her home. So, after making a couple of suggestions, which he shot down for various reasons I told him that he couldn't go wrong with something from Victoria Secrets. After all, what woman doesn't want something silky, soft and fluffy or some smell-good, nice lingerie—bathrobe or whatever?

Eagerly I told her of the suggestions I'd made and for her to expect some pretty and soft things under the tree. To my dismay, she quickly retorted, "I don't want something from Victoria Secrets. That would be a gift for him, not for me." I was surprised at her response, to say the least, but I quickly assessed that this was a woman who didn't trust her man. Whenever a woman doesn't want to be intimate with the man in her life it's because she doesn't trust him on some level. I felt a little bad, and we sort of laughed it off as I told her I wasn't sure if he even took my suggestion, but if he had, to get ready to make some returns.

Charla and Tony had only been married a couple of years and had gotten married immediately after her father, who had taken great care of her, passed away. From outside appearances they seemed to fit together so well.

It was the following summer when Charla came in asking me if I knew a certain woman. After a little back and forth, and separation by a degree or two, I revealed that I did know whom she was speaking of. I couldn't imagine why she would be asking about this person because they were certainly from two different circles. Charla went on to tell me she had discovered that Tony had been consorting with this person. Surely not, was my answer.

To cut across the field—Tony eventually left Charla for this woman who was, to be nice, less than average looking (I don't mean God-given looks, I mean personal upkeep), living in a run down Section-

8 home with a bunch of small children (not his). After trying to reassure her that surely he wasn't interested in this other woman over her, we were both (and everyone else that bared witness) flabbergasted when he moved in — and eventually married her.

Speechless was what I was. Never in a million years would I have guessed this would possibly be the outcome. For the longest time I tried figuring this thing out on my own. I was fresh out of advice. But I did later surmise that Tony didn't feel needed or appreciated by Charla — or at least not in the way that he needed to be needed and appreciated. The home they lived in, she owned (nice and fully furnished), she had two children left at home that were well taken care of by her.

> *In fact, legalizing polygamy is something that should be seriously considered.*

I'm not saying that a woman has to be broke, busted and disgusted before she can have a man but a he needs to feel necessary in her life and he needs to know that he can bring her pleasure in some way.

Being in a relationship is not so much about how you feel about another person — it's about how the other person makes you feel about yourself when you're with them. Does being around this man make you feel feminine, pretty, or smart? Does being around you make him feel like a man, strong and capable?

This situation taught me a lot about people and their needs and how they are not all the same. No matter what we thought about Tony's needs and who we thought he was as a person, he knew what he wanted and what made him happy.

I really wouldn't mind having a husband, but...

The duties of a wife are some of the most un-gratifying, un-notarized and unfulfilling duties of any job there is. Even if notoriety and gratification are not the motivation in a marriage everyone needs validation on some level to stay in the game and keep going. If you're not called to the position of wife, but end up on the job, it will be down right arduous.

I really wouldn't mind having a husband, but I'm just not that interested in being someone's wife. There is just way too much work involved.

In fact, legalizing polygamy is something that should be seriously considered. Yes, you heard me right. I'm not speaking of course, of those situations where women are brainwashed, or children and young girls are being sexually abused.

I'm referring specifically to men who first of all have the mental capacity and maturity, not to mention the financial means, to take care of more than one wife and multiple children.

If this admission just blew your hair back, feel free to skip ahead to the next section.

This is not a solution for everyone because many people would not be mature enough or have the level of self-assurance to engage in such a practice. Might I also add, some do not have the desire to take part in a group marriage.

When maintaining multiple relationships I'm speaking of men. This may sound one sided and again, sexist, but for the most part women don't generally have the capacity or the desire for multiple relationships with several men, but men on the other hand are designed to, and have the constant desires to seek out multiple women. It's basic logic and biology not to mention biblical.

There are many reasons I believe polygamy should be considered beginning with basic math. If you examine the ratio between marriageable men and marriageable women you will discover the two come nowhere close to being balanced. And for those of you who think I'm suggesting something real crazy, consider this; it is not a crime for a man to go from woman to woman having sex, and even impregnating them. But when a man wants to sanctify his relationships with women by marrying and providing for them, it becomes a crime. There is something a little twisted behind that logic – I'm just sayin'.

"Although, newer studies are showing that much younger generations are proving to be more equally balanced, currently there are seven women to one man in the Black community. The nation's male population grew at a slightly faster rate (13.9 percent) than the female population (12.5 percent) over the last decade of the 20th century, resulting in a lessening of the gap between the number of men and women." This is according to new analysis released by the Commerce Department's Census Bureau, which unfortunately means little to those of us who are more than 17 years of age.

The statistics also show that in the age category from 20s to 30s, there are currently 115 unmarried men for every 100 women; but in the 45 to 64 age-range, there are only 69 unmarried men for every 100 women. This gap is even wider for Black male and females—and let's face it, most black women want a black man.

Because the ratio is basically even at the time of birth the men, apparently, are dropping like flies, while women evidently, live longer lives.

Throughout the Bible you don't find God instructing men to have only one wife but you read where Jesus calls out the woman at the well about all of her husbands [John 4:16-18].

To quote Q from the movie The Best Man (not verbatim): "Why would God give us [men] all this sperm, and why would [women] out number us the way that they do if men were supposed to be monoga- mous?" Self-serving as it were, you must admit he had a point. I must add; I don't be- lieve *every* man has the desire or emotional wherewithal for multiple relationships, but it be a viable solution for many men and women.

> *The virtuous woman during a twelve-hour day basically lined up the planets in the universe, put out the fires in hell, then at least one time walked the circumference of the earth and all this before lunch.*

There is a saying that any women can bring a man to a climax but not any man can make a woman climax? We all know how true this is. When a man is doing his job and doing it (and doing it and doing it) well, we really don't crave other male attention. But, most men constantly crave female attention and rarely can one woman satisfy the urge for long.

The next reason is attributed to the amount of labor that rests on the shoulders of the wife and mother. Exhibit A: Proverbs 31:10. The virtuous woman during a twelve-hour day basically lined up the planets in the universe, put out the fires in hell, then at least one time walked the circumference of the earth and all this before lunch. Okay, not quite, but…

When my former husband and I did our pre-marital counseling, marginal as it was, that was one of the scriptures I was instructed to read (I don't remember which scripture he was assigned to read or if he was even assigned one) and one of the things which sticks out in my memory was how I felt after I read this scripture: my first feeling was, exhaustion, and then wonderment on what was that husband of hers doing all day. I felt certain he hadn't worked half as hard on his J.O.B as she had on hers.

I also considered the fact that the scripture doesn't mention after all she did she still had to end her evening satisfying her husband. Uhmm.

If a woman is mature enough to handle letting some one else take on some of her marital duties and she is sincerely interested in lightening her load than she may see how the institution of polygamy could be beneficial.

Working a full time job, keeping a perfect house and raising intelligent, well-rounded and healthy children in addition to keeping your husband sexually fulfilled is enough to make any wife desperate.

Polygamy is another assignment you must be called for in order for it to be successful. Just as we have a choice to remain single or get married, being apart of a group marriage would be a choice as well.

Funny but true:

Married men live longer than single men do, but married men are a lot more willing to die.

Single women live longer than married women, but married women are much more willing to commit murder.

That was to make you chuckle but there is scientific proof on the longevity of life where married and single people are concerned. One quote I like to reflect on often is that of the Delaney sisters who both lived several years past their 100th birthdays, when they said the reason they'd lived so long was because they didn't have a man worrying them to death[2]. Neither had ever married.

"One of the things I noticed early in my practice is that the people who are the most chronically ill are often people who have a great deal of emotional hurt in their past.

"The examples are many. The woman who has had numerous back surgeries and has a number of debilitating problems who was in an extremely abusive marriage, which involved repeated rape and sexual abuse. The soft-spoken, shy woman who struggles with pelvic pain was sexually abused every Sunday morning by her father (a minister) before he went to preach." Dr. Jill Waggoner, author of *My Sister's Keeper: Is Your Temple In Order?*[3] gives insight, as extreme as they maybe, on toxic relationships and emotional wounds.

If it appears as though I'm giving conflicting advice it's because I encourage every woman to embrace the ideas of both being married and being single, further more, to be realistic about both.

"This above all: To thine ownself be true, and it must follow, as the night the day, thou canst not then be false to any man."[4] This is a quote from the William Shakespeare play, Hamlet, Act 1 Scene 3, and can be interpreted in different ways but I believe it means once you find a way to be true to yourself it will be impossible to then live a lie.

> *The next time you find yourself in the company of someone that makes you question how you got there, ask yourself what it was about you that attracted such a person.*

If God has called you to marriage then you should prepare yourself as potential wife material. But as a single woman you shouldn't just automatically assume that marriage is just another step in the progression of life. And, if wedded bliss is not your calling, to find happiness in this and great satisfaction in the beauty of singleness. Find your own truth.

When we choose a spouse:

Men and women alike marry whatever their issue was growing up. And the reason they subconsciously do this is because they are trying to fix or heal the unresolved relationship. If a man grew up with a female figure—say, his mother—that was contingent or dependent then he marries a woman who displays the same trait because he's trying to repair the first relationship.

When a woman grows up with a father who, for instance was an alcoholic she will forever be attracted to men who have an addiction. Usually it will be a different addiction because she may have told herself she would never end up with a man like her father but she simply traded in one addiction for another.

In order to avoid this you must make a conscious effort to recognize what your issues may be, by being real with yourself and figuring out why you make the decisions you do when choosing a mate.

Have you ever asked yourself why you continue to end up with the same kind of men over and over? You have to change your pattern and your taste in men. The next time you find yourself in the company of someone that makes you question how you got there, ask yourself what it was about *you* that attracted such a person.

Defining Your Own Idea of Success:

Admiring other couples from afar can be misleading. When you see them out in public it's only natural that they're on their best behavior; loving and respectful of each others needs. If this is a couple you are close to, you may find upon closer inspection they are not exactly who you thought they were when you first met them.

This doesn't mean they don't have a successful marriage but it may not be successful according to your standards.

1. Are you admiring couples needlessly?
2. Do you understand what your own standards are?
3. What is your personal definition of success?
4. How do you define a successful marriage?

Before you can find success you must be able to define it for yourself. The couple or couples you are admiring may have a different measuring stick than you do. A husband who simply brings home a regular paycheck may be the only prerequisite to a winning marriage for some women just as a having a beautiful woman with a fit body as a wife may be the definition of a healthy union for some men.

Section End:
Questions and other things to consider:

1. What are your true expectations of a husband?
2. What do you believe should be expected of you as a wife?
3. For a moment, realistically analyze your behavior in past relationships and your role in the break up of each one.
4. Are you overly critical where others are concerned?
5. Do you constantly end up in relationships with overly critical people?
6. Have you ever been afraid to reveal your true self in a relationship?
7. What does true intimacy mean to you?
8. What are your issues from childhood or adolescence?
9. Develop your own measuring stick of what a successful relationship or marriage should look like.

Write down or journal your thoughts so that you may develop a good sense of self, your desires and your expectations.

Section 3

Marriage is for the Grown & Sexy

Marriage License: Only the mature need apply.

Remember the woman who placed the ad in the paper which read, "Looking for the man of my dreams. He's the man that would never hit me. He would never leave me and he can satisfy me in bed."

One month later her bell rings and a quadriplegic man is at the door announcing himself as the 'man of her dreams'. With a quizzical look on her face she questions him as to how he could possibly be the man of her dreams only to have him reply "Well, I have no arms so I will never hit you and I have no legs so I can never leave you."

After considering this for a moment she asks him "But, can you satisfy me in bed?" he answers, "How do you think I rang the doorbell."

A man with no arms could never physically strike out but, this speaks nothing to verbal abuse, which is just as damaging, if not more so than a black eye and a bruised rib. Mental abuse takes years and a lot of hard work to overcome and regain self-esteem and self-worth. And many people never recover completely and live many years never believing themselves worthy of good love and healthy relationships.

And a man who isn't able to pick 'em up and put 'em down can still walk out emotionally, which can be far worse than coming home and finding an empty space in the closet. There are few things sadder than having someone around that you fail to connect with on any level.

Believing that sex is a foundation for a good marriage is certainly an immature attitude. And thinking that sex has everything to do with the body is ignore-ance. Sex (or at least good sex) is mostly mental, spiritual and emotional.

> *Having unrealistic expectations of ourselves and other people is counter-productive and simply put, makes life much harder to live.*

The joke at the opening of this section spotlights how a lot of women rationalize in this same way. Biblically speaking a man is supposed to be *finding* his wife, not a woman *finding* her husband. The sad truth is, while looking for a husband, women really want a project to work on and aren't really interested in partnering up with a man and becoming his helpmeet. Women are natural born nurturers; this is how they express their love.

A woman with control issues is constantly looking for things she can take charge of. So she may set out looking for a man down on his luck who will become dependent upon her. Then, she'll put him in a position where he's stuck. Remember the song by the Ohio Players, *I Want To Be Free* (some of you young 'uns will have to look this up)? It's about a man who is whining and crying about wanting to get away from his controlling woman but is stuck like chuck, which is exactly the position a controlling woman wants her man in.

Confusing reality with fantasy

One of the worst mistakes a woman can make is to, in her mind, turn a situation from what it really is into what she wants it to be. Confusing fantasy with reality.

Years ago, I had just begun seeing this guy I was really digging. We had known each other as friends for a long time but we were in our early stages of dating. The night that Carl, we'll call him, and I were consummating our relationship he made it *perfectly* clear he still loved his ex-wife and always would no matter what happened in the future. Instead of me recognizing this as a red flag and backing up out of that situation I foolishly, because I wanted him so bad (so I thought), continued on as if he hadn't said a word.

I convinced myself that the way Carl felt about her wouldn't affect the outcome of my relationship with him. In fact I believed that in no time he would forget all about her. Hey, I was over my ex so eventually he'd get over his too.

Instead of hearing what he was trying to tell me I totally disregarded everything he said. I filed the information in the back of my mind, but I didn't really think it would mean anything in the long run. I went on with my own fantasy and made myself totally available to him.

Carl didn't have to do a lick of work to get me or keep me around. It worked for a while but as time moved on, of course we realized that we were both packing too much baggage to try and build a relationship together.

He never did get back with his ex, but he didn't make it with me either. No bad break up, we just moved on. Years later when I teasingly reminded him of his earlier profession he didn't believe he could have ever spoken anything resembling those sentiments. And even though I disregarded it I remembered very well what he had said to me as I sat there on his bed in my unmentionables as he declared an undying love over another woman. What an idiot I was!

> There should be laws passed to make marriage harder to get in to but easier to get out of.

In retrospect, I don't really believe I reacted this way because of how I felt about him it was because I had an idea in my head of how I wanted things to turn out, which goes back to the false realities we women create and latch on to.

Once we make it a habit of dealing with what's real and facing the realities of life no matter how harsh they may be, we will be happier, more well-rounded people. Having unrealistic expectations of ourselves and other people is counter-productive and simply put, makes life much harder to live.

Hard to get in to and easy to get out of

There should be laws passed to make marriage harder to get in to but easier to get out of. In a perfect world a woman would meet Mr. Right, fall in love at first sight and once he announced his undying love for her too they'd spend a short romantic time together and then march right into marital bliss and live happily ever after.

Of course it doesn't work this way at all but so many men and women still think it's still possible and probable. I believe if marriages were a little more difficult to get into the divorce rate would be on a steady decline.

For instance, if there were classes that a couple was ordered to take, similar to Lamaze or Child Develop-ment, or a mandatory six-month (at least) waiting period it would make all the difference. Then, after going through all of that if the marriage didn't work out it should be as simple as one, two, three to get out of instead of a long, ugly court battle.

This would also cut down on couples feeling compelled, out of guilt or pressure to remain miserable in loveless marriages.

Understanding Men

It seems as though there are so many books and reference tools out there to assist women with understanding men but I struggle to find books for men on learning the ways of women. Maybe they're out there—deeply buried under all the ones for women. This issue hits a sore spot with me especially the ones written for women by men. *Checkmate: The Games Men Play,* by Mark Crutcher, *Getting and Keeping Your Mate "Trained," "Whipped," Faithful," and on a "Leash!!"* by Brittian Wilder III, and *If You Want Closure In Your Relationship, Start With Your Legs*, by Big Boom, and of course, *Act Like a Lady, Think Like a Man,* by Steve Harvey, are just a few that I find offensive.

It's not the messages in the books it's the idea of the books in the first place. Why don't these men get busy offering up advice to men? And really, are they giving women advice or bragging about their exploits? Men are writing books for women and women are writing books for women. Why is there no one writing books for all the knuckleheads out there? Probably because they don't read! Aghh! But, I digress.

Having a healthy understanding of men is essential to being a mature woman. Don't think like a man, understand how men think. Whether you decide to be in a relationship or not it's a good idea to get this understanding. As I mentioned before, one of the biggest problems between men and women is each group not appreciating or understanding the other. The two sexes are attracted to each other but rarely ever take the time to gain an understanding or realize the true core differences of each other.

According to Sheron Patterson in *Put On Your Crown: The Black Woman's Guide to Living Single (... and Christian)*, "There are two common mistakes women make in their understanding of men. First, they erroneously elevate them [men] to the level of gods, or second they denigrate men to the level of sugar daddies."[5]

> *If you have a tendency to get into friendships or date men who dominate or control you, this will continue to happen until you learn the lesson you're supposed to learn.*

Although different from us, they are mere human beings. Men display heroic characteristics but they were not put on this earth to save us. We love the fairytales and playing the damsel in distress but if you are a Christian then you know Jesus is your all in all Savior.

Expecting a man to be an automated teller machine also is not only wrong it leaves both sides with their self worth and self image injured. A man is reduced to his monetary worth and the woman will struggle to have a positive outlook when her man is feeling worthless.

Learning the Lessons

The average woman will admit that she has done her fair share of dating; and for some, *more* than her fair share. She may even admit that it seems she continuously dates the same kind of man or has the same experiences over and over. It is no accident that we attract certain elements.

Until we pass the test we will have to continue to retake it. This is advice for any relationship we may encounter. If you have a tendency to get into friendships or date men who dominate or control you, this will continue to happen until you learn the lesson you're supposed to learn. None of this is by accident, happenstance or coincidence. God (the Universe) is trying to teach you something. And, the lesson for you to learn may be different from others who are in your same situation.

"Some of us, for example, might experience one such impediment as the inability to forgive; if so, we will attract experiences that will give us ample opportunity to either hold a grudge or forgive. Others of us might tend to be selfish, or controlling such instances would "call" for the universe to keep providing us with opportunities which would tempt us to be tightfisted or bossy… or we will make the shift and begin to respond to life in a more evolved manner."[6] This is an excerpt from *The One: Finding Soul Mate Love And Making It Last,* by Kathy Freston.

When you are working to break a cycle of say, repeatedly dating men who cheat on you, doing things differently is not always enough. You need to educate yourself about what happened in the past relationship and why you behaved in the manner you did—learn the lesson.

Big Boom, author of *If You Want Closure In Your Relationship, Start With Your Legs* says, "Having sex with the closing partner [the partner she is trying to

I Wouldn't Mind Having A Husband · 53

gain closure with] not only opens her legs, it opens emotional doors for a woman, and both should remain closed to allow that flame to die."[7] With all due respect, this sounds good but until you've learned the lesson you will, no matter how hard you try, still deal with the situation or another one identical to it until the lesson, whatever it is, is learned. If you're in a relationship that needs to end, I say stay in it until you get so fed up with it you won't ever want to be bothered with anything that resembles it ever again.

Stella, a good friend and former client of mine is a recovering drug addict. A program she was ordered to attend because of some other trouble she had gotten into was after she had been clean for some time. One day she was discussing one of her sessions with me and expressed her impatience with the other recovering participants. She didn't understand why they just didn't stop slipping back. I had naively had that attitude in the past about former addicts but was surprised to hear her have the same sentiments. So I filled in the void and took on the advocate role when asking her why she was being so harsh. I thought she of all people would understand, if not sympathize with the backsliding of an addict.

Stella said, pretty much in a nutshell, that she smoked crack for years and did the low-down things crack addicts do and one day she got tired of living like that and she quit. That was it for her. No going back. No relapses. She just stopped. So, she felt like that's what others should do. I guess that's what they call hitting rock bottom.

Until you arrive at the place where you're finally learning the lesson your behavior will continue. The longer it takes you to get it, the longer you stay in the tailspin.

Section End:

Questions to ponder and consider.

1. Is sex your number one reason for wanting to be married?
2. Are you attracted to men who need some fixing up or that you can turn into a project?
3. Do you have fairytale issues?
4. Based on the repeated struggles you've had in your life, what lessons do you believe God is trying to teach you? List them.
5. Do you find yourself falling in love easily?
6. Is your love for other people always contingent upon how they treat you?

Be honest with yourself on your patterns and habits of falling in love. It takes courage to be realistic and to take a truthful inner look.

Section 4

The Divorce from Hell

Little lies.

No one sets out in marriage contemplating a divorce. But, what if you did? Not in a morbid sort of way where you're setting yourself up with a death wish (speaking to the death of a marriage) but, in a realistic way of thinking of an 'every' case scenario. Ask yourself, "How would this man treat me during a divorce?"

This is something most people don't consider. And when the person you were supposed to love forever, turns into public enemy number it's difficult to process. When the man who was supposed to honor and cherish you is not only *not* wishing you well but is doing everything within his power to bring you down it's enough to literally change your outlook on life, love and relationships. You lose faith in romance and commitment. Say you pledged your life to a man who seems to be out to get you. The word "committed" will take on a whole new meaning—complete with straitjacket.

When you're romantically involved in the beginning and still feeling the fluttering wings of butterflies in your stomach you would never guess that this same person would later call you out of your name, disrespect you in ways you would never imagine, plot against you, and sometimes even strike you.

If you pay attention, there are always signs early on. For instance, I was talking to a guy on the phone for the first time. We were introduced through one of my family members and he was another one who looked good on paper. During this first conversation he tells me how much he hates his brother's wife and then calls her a beyotch (the first time I'd ever heard the term). I knew at that moment if not any other,

> *There was also a time when I believed you had to choose between love and marriage. You could not have both. You could have one and then the other but never both together.*

he wasn't the one for me. Any man that would think it okay to call a woman out of her name will one day think it okay to do the same to me. Eww! And how unattractive is that anyway?

It's the little things in the beginning, which lead up to the big things later. Small incidences that may not seem to mean much early on, fester and grow into bigger things or make it easier to get to the more hurtful things.

By the time you reach the courtroom you are so used to saying ugly words that both of you are spitting out hateful retorts at each other and wondering how you got there when you once thought you were so in love.

Love and romance

Love is a verb or an action, not an emotion, as many of us have believed or was taught. That thing we feel is simple attraction.

Most people believe hate to be the opposite of love, but actually the opposite of love is indifference. Think about it. Love is a choice you make and not an emotion you have. Love is a choice you make to care about something or someone and when you don't love something you are indifferent towards it. When making the choice to love, it's easier to when it's something or someone you feel some attraction towards.

Women in general are still optimistic and encouraged about love, romance and marriage, if you can group those three together. There was a time when I would have believed marriage to be the odd ball out. There was also a time when I believed you had to choose between love and marriage. You could not have both. You could have one and then the other but never both together.

I no longer believe this but the notion still lingers in the recesses of my mind. As a Christian I know it was never God's intention for two people, once so in love, to turn into archenemies. If marriage is your calling and you wait upon the Lord, He will grant you such desires.

The reason I believe couples lose focus on the romance of their relationship is because once they're married they get busy with the business of life and forget all about each other's personal or romantic needs.

Deep down women really want love and romance but they have been conditioned or tricked, if you will, into thinking they want marriage further believing they have to have marriage in order to have love and romance. Romance, love, marriage and security are also not necessarily systematic. How lovely life would be if they were.

Security; what is it? Unfortunately Black women of today have rarely experienced such an anomaly. Depending on your own definition of being or feeling secure you will find this rarely exists.

There are many women who can honestly say they have never felt safe in the presence of any man. They didn't have a father in the home, or a healthy example of a father figure, and every man they were romantically involved with wronged them in some way. If they stretched their memories they may recall someone—a distant uncle, coach or teacher but never anyone in close proximity—that meant them well.

In fact, I would venture to say I'm one of those women. When I say "safe", I don't mean I necessarily feared for my life, per se, with the men in my life, but I don't know of a man who truly wished me well or one who wouldn't hesitate to give his life for me— except for The One who already has. I know there are women out there whose experience differ from mine and probably feel sad for me and other women like me, as they should, because it's a sad reality.

Some time ago I met a popular Christian Fiction, author who said, in her books she writes about good men who are always employed and respectful towards women. She said, this is her own personal reality and when one of her readers asked about this, she simply answered that all the men in her life — her father, husband, and others — have all been admirable men and like any writer, it's difficult to write about things that aren't your reality.

For a brief moment I was jealous of her — and maybe didn't quite believe her. Once the moment passed it came to my realization that there are most certainly plenty of women with her same experiences, however there are far too many if not more women with my experience where we struggle to name adequate or admirable men within close personal, proximity.

Languages of love

A few years back I was in a relationship when I felt really loved. It was amazing to me because it was the first time as a full-fledged adult I'd felt this way. In most every other area the thing was dysfunctional but I felt truly loved and here's the reason why.

Sometime later after the relationship ended, I read The Five Love Languages by Gary Chapman and there within the pages of his book a revelation happened. Not only did I discover why I'd felt so loved in this particular relationship I realized why I hadn't felt that way before in other relationships.

Chapman says that we all speak or communicate love in our own ways. The five love languages are 1) Words of Affirmation, 2) Quality Time, 3) Receiving of Gifts, 4) Acts of Service, 5) Physical Touch[8].

Reading the book it was clear to me my own love language was Acts of Service and this was the reason I felt, or didn't feel loved based on said need being met or not. It was clear that, I'll call him Anthony, caught on fairly quickly what put a smile on my face. This was when he did things for me. He was very intuitive in this way.

Anthony hadn't read the book but he had the concept down. He knew that anything he could do to make life easier for me was what put me at ease so it's what he did. I'd come home to the grass being cut or the garage cleaned out. He put gas in my car, brought lunch or had it delivered to me at the salon, and he even fixed my clothes dryer. No one had ever loved me the way he had. He took care of things before I had to ask and things I didn't even know needed taken care of.

Anthony's own love language was physical touch, which became obvious to me once I completely understood the message in the book. I am not a touchy-feely person and Anthony was very openly affectionate. There were times when he'd ask me why I didn't touch him more. I told him it just didn't come natural to

> *A woman needs a man who can lead. And when a man cannot lead it's just the beginning of a plethora of problems for a couple.*

me. Once when he was sleeping our arms were resting against each other's when I shifted and pulled away his breathing rate increased. I took my hand and touched his arm and it slowed down. I removed my hand and put it back several times trying to see if it were just a fluke. It was amazing to me, his need for connectedness.

Those on the outside thought we were a mismatched couple based on some of the many differences between us but I felt as though we were the perfect fit. I had never had anyone work so hard to make me happy. Because a huge void was being filled within me I was slow to recognize how toxic everything else was.

We had figured out how to make each other feel loved but it wasn't enough to overcome the other obstacles we faced. Even though things eventually ended I was still very excited to learn this about myself as well as how important it is to learn someone else's love language.

Following the Leader

A woman needs a man who can lead. And when a man cannot lead it's just the beginning of a plethora of problems for a couple. Again, this all may sound sexist but I really do feel as though as time has marched on women have stepped out of place.

When we try to do it all, as women, there is always some area that will suffer. Sarah Palin trying to balance a marriage, five children, and the whole state of Alaska—on her way to becoming Vice

President was a disaster waiting to happen. I'm not saying she isn't capable of working outside the home, but running our country—I doubt it. So many women are out of order but it's simply because men aren't doing what they should be doing.

Men should lead. It's so simple and if women are honest they'll admit they're much happier beings when men are leading—in love, of course. I am not speaking of men who rule over women with an iron fist; I'm talking about with total reverence and devotion for women.

Society as a whole—not just in the Black community—has gotten out of order. But, especially in our community women are taking over. And if we view it from a perspective of cause and effect, I have surmised, that women are out of order because men have been out of order.

"I believe that the main reason why many of us as young black men do not have a healthy attitude towards self-responsibility," says, Daniel Whyte III, in *Letter To Young Black Men: Advice And Encouragement For A Difficult Journey*, "is because we have never been taught it, and because we have not seen it exemplified by many older black men. Most of us have seen our black women take responsibility, but seldom have we seen our black men do so. This is a tragedy."[9]

Early in 2007, CBS canceled the controversial radio show, hosted by Don Imus, when he denigrated the women of the Rutgers University Women's Basketball team on the air (regardless of the fact he'd been doing this for years). This prompted many people to take a look into Rappers who speak the same misogynistic language as the infamous sports radio personality.

Before Imus was officially fired, Oprah Winfrey invited many guests on to voice their opinions on the topic that was at the top of everyone's discussion list, including the syndicated columnist for *The New York Daily News*, Stanley Crouch. While watching the show I witnessed Mr. Crouch become irate as his emotions segued into frustration. I then heard him say something that got me hotter than fish grease. As the heated discussion moved from Imus to the many Rappers—Russell Simmons, Common and Kevin Liles, there to somewhat speak on their behalf—Mr. Crouch blurted out that women needed to head up the movement to address the issue of the many Rappers who have become very comfortable calling them bitches and hoes in their music on the regular.

> *In any relationship whether it is between a parent and child, male and female or a platonic friendship it is human nature to*

My question is; why are men so willing to sit back and let us women clean up their messes? Is it because they're so used to us handling the business? Is it because we have a society full of pitiful, sorry-ass Black men? No, it's because of a process which has taken place so slowly and has been going on for so long we haven't a clue as to how to fix it and have just accepted things as they are.

To prove to you this was not an isolated case, in Dallas there was a protest on certain radio stations, which habitually play rap music with denigrating lyrics. This protest was to put pressure on the stations and enforce cleaner music for the public. Originally, the plan was to let the women head it up but as an afterthought some men finally came to their senses and decided men needed to at least join them. Why was there a delay? Why was it not an immediate action — or reaction for the men to take on this plight?

Black women in America have not had the luxury of our men speaking up for us or regularly coming to our rescue. This has left us to speak up for ourselves — in turn making us mouthy, domineering and too outspoken. It's because we are attempting to fill in the void.

In any relationship whether it is between a parent and child, male and female or a platonic friendship it is human nature to fill in voids. When there is a parent who acts dependent you find the child acting more like a parent, which is out of order, but it's a yearning in the human spirit to have balance. And because our men have been out of order for centuries in this country the black woman has mutated into something that was once self-preservation into our biggest personal downfall.

Mixed into the equation are many generations of men who were raised by women. These boys grow into men suffering the inner turmoil of trying to be men while lacking the training, which would've come from the men in their lives. In addition, they are castrated by dominating women.

Even though we have never really had the feeling of being taken care of by our men women still, for the most part desire them to do so. It's a fundamental urge. We have turned bitter, angry and sometimes hard to love because of the inner knowledge we have that the innate need to be protected and cared for won't be met.

Our attitudes have become sour, distasteful, vicious, ruthless and distressing. Our behavior has evolved into something peculiar and we do these odd things because of the breakdown. When women adapt to not having the support of their men, their behavior becomes unrecognizable.

Let's look at Lot. In Genesis 19:6 he offers up his young virgin daughters to a crowd of perverts. For these to know that their father, the one who was supposed to give his own life to protect them, was willing to hand them over to be raped had to be a horrible realization. Twisted in his mind, he may have thought he was doing something great by protecting the angels God had sent but as it is said, the road to hell is paved with good intentions.

We look ahead to Genesis 19:30 where Lot's daughters get him drunk and rape him. I am convinced those two incidences are directly related. Perversion follows more perversion.

So, before black men go bad mouthing us, saying we talk too much, were too loud or speak out of turn they should consider we speak up too much because they don't speak up at all.

Section End:

Things to reflect on:

1. Do you feel divorce is an easy fix for a marriage gone badly or do you believe divorce should rarely or never be considered?
2. Do you find that you have become increasingly angry or resentful the longer you remain single?
3. List the men in your life who you believe to be trustworthy or who you feel safe in their presence.
4. List the relationships, platonic or romantic, in which you have experienced the void filling process.
5. Do you see yourself as one of the dominant, outspoken women described in this section?

Consider the lists you make and your answers to help you draw conclusions on your true feeling on marriage and singleness.

Section 5

Single, Saved, and Sexually Satisfied

How important is sex?

Depriving the body of sex is unnatural. Celibacy can be equated to anorexia. Humans crave five things 1) food 2) water 3) air 4) sleep 5) sex. Imagine how you would function if your body went without sleep for an extended amount of time. What about food, water or air? As a Christian, I'm sure others in the faith may see this line of thinking as going against God as well as promoting sexual sins. My motivation is not to change a person's views if they believe sex outside of marriage is a sin. Actually, I agree. I just believe it's no greater sin than gossiping or lying, as an example.

There aren't any bigger consequences to suffer because of sex outside of marriage than there is stealing, lying or murder.

Throughout history, society has associated such shame with babies being born out of wedlock and adultery when gossiping and lying has a far greater reach of hurt and damage. A sharp tongue can do way more damage than most any other sin. The affects are so far reaching that the chain reaction can hardly be measured.

The Act of Marriage: The Beauty of Sexual Love, by Tim & Beverly LaHaye, sites, "God obviously had many purposes in mind when He deliberately created our sexual capabilities, from reproduction to pleasure to unique union. Like all things He created, it is all very good… All people have the same choice about the use of their sex drive. They can obey God and confine its expression to marriage, which He calls sacred, or they can adopt the standards of the world and… become promiscuous."[11]

For those of you who think you are damning yourselves to hell if you have sex outside of marriage I would be the last one to persuade you otherwise. But, if you have accepted Christ in your life, your assurance of salvation is found in Romans 8:29-39, *And those he predestined, he also called; those he called, he also justified; those he justified, he also glorified.* When you accepted Christ, he had already accepted you; you were answering his beckoning. God reached out to you first. So, it was predestined that you would belong to the Kingdom.

I have never been one to beat people over the head with the Bible. Everyone has their own frame of references to come to their own conclusions (hopefully guided by the Holy Spirit), which makes them who they are. Looking at this thing realistically and knowing that so many women will not be walking down the aisle, whether it is their choice or not, I hesitate to encourage a life of celibacy. I feel such a movement on a grand scale can easily morph into an action of lesbianism or possibly other perverted sins.

There is divine providence behind those who are chosen by God to practice celibacy. I believe He places a special ability in those such as monks, nuns, and others whom He has called for such a purpose.

Have you ever gotten real with God? He created your body. He knows and understands it better than you do. Talk with Him about His plans for you. He knows what you can and cannot handle and He knows your heart and intentions.

> *Sex can be like a reflex in the right situation. And that's exactly what happened to all of the women who became pregnant while not having sex—pun intended.*

I have had many single girlfriends become pregnant during spans of abstaining. Seriously. I have one friend who was going around professing to people that she was no longer having sex. In fact anyone who would listen she'd tell them. I asked her why she felt the need to announce it to the world and she replied it was for accountability reasons. She believed it would help her remain true to the commitment she'd made. I advised her to stop because I believed it would make things more difficult for her. It would be too much pressure.

Sex can be like a reflex in the right situation. And that's exactly what happened to all of the women who became pregnant while not having sex—pun intended.

My friends, who I'm speaking of, believed themselves so committed to the new lifestyle; they stopped taking care of their business and in one act of heated passion, "Wham."

Can you imagine how they must have felt when they had to tell those they'd professed to, they were now having a baby? Or those who later seen them with swollen bellies who'd heard them say they were no longer having sex. For many women abstaining from sex, it's like saying you are never going to think another bad thought. Unless there is a physiological reason, I don't believe the majority of people who claim to not be having sex really aren't.

I would be the last person to tell a woman not to get her swerve on but the first to tell her to be sexually responsible by taking care of and protecting herself. Also, I'd tell her to make smart choices and be true to her own self.

The advice given in this section is for those with healthy views on sex and sexuality. It is not for women who may have been abused or molested where frigidness or promiscuity is an issue for them. This is for women who have healthy or normal sex-drives but realize getting married may not happen.

Sexually Secure

I have always admired any female who was secure with her sexuality and believe most women if not all have hoe tendencies whether they believe it or not. Before you are offended by the word, just consider the meaning of the term — whore or harlot — whichever word you prefer to use. According to definition, she is a woman who gives sex or sexual favors in exchange for gifts, money, financial security and most any other thing.

It is no secret that sexually active women (of all ages) at some point have had sex with men in exchange for something. It is most likely a subconscious act and is exchanged almost innocently, if you will—meals, gifts, bills paid. And wives are guilty of this as well.

Men are mostly motivated to have sex biologically and for the pure sake of having sex. When in a relationship, unlike men, women are motivated to have sex for reasons outside of the simple desire to have sex (those dynamics are changing as more women take on male-like personas). It's in exchange for love or simply to satisfy the man. And therein lies the problem.

When the exchange doesn't work out for whatever reason women are left feeling used and men are left feeling confused. A woman in her frustration will either get religious or take a vow of celibacy, or both. I've seen it more times than I can count. Not to mention the times I, myself have traveled the same road.

If you can relate then you know the defeat and dejection you feel when you find that you failed to conquer such a difficult feat. Women don't get the relationship they sought and men don't get the unattached sex they were hoping for.

Self-Worth, Self-Respect, and Self-Esteem

Before you can make healthy choices, you must have your self-esteem in tact.

If you are easily infatuated, become obsessed in relationships or have misguided intentions, you may want to check out how you really feel about yourself and what you believe yourself to be worthy of. Infatuations are—as was mentioned in Section 3— unrealistic expectations. Stop looking at every man as a potential husband. In fact, stop obsessing over having a husband—wedding or whatever you obsess over. Some women are so desperate to get married, instead of thinking about the kind of life they would want if they were to marry, they try and fit themselves into the many different lives of the men they run across.

If a capricious woman meets a guy who lives on a ranch, she will envision her life as the wife of a cowboy. Five minutes later this same woman will see a corporate attorney and imagine a high profile life living in the city with this man. She does this constantly because practically any man will do—she just wants to be married.

Obsessive women are so afraid to be alone, when they're in a relationship they end up sabotaging it out of fear. They think every other woman is more worthy than they are and think so little of themselves they can't imagine a man really being interested in them. They worry about being smart enough, or become intimidated by other women, or obsess over their bodies or appearance. This is all in respect to what women think men are thinking about them instead of what they think of themselves. Women give men way too much power.

David Zinczenko's book, *Men, Love & Sex*, tells us what men really think, "Your body is all about feel: How you feel about it, and how often we [men] can feel it."[12]

It's not just about your insecurities. Do you look forward to the future or do you mostly cling to the past? When you are around outgoing, intelligent people do you shrink to the back of the room? Do you feel you add

> *To improve your self-esteem you must first resist the inner voice that feeds you negative images of yourself.*

value to social situations? When someone praises you for your work do you diminish the compliment or hesitate before saying thank you? Does your inner voice criticize you often or lift you up?

Low self-esteem is not always easy to recognize. When we see a woman behaving in a self-destructive manner, disrespecting herself and others around her, we know she has self-worth issues. We may think, after seeing other women acting out, our own self-esteem is in check. After all, we aren't hooked on drugs, we'd never let a man beat us or verbally abuse us. In fact, we don't take crap from anybody. Before you pat yourself on the back:

What would happen if you didn't compare yourself to other women? Would your "self-esteem radar" be at its full potential?

The Counseling & Mental Health Center at The University of Texas in Austin, says there are three faces of low self-esteem: The Imposter, The Rebel and The Loser. You may think you're in good standing but these traits aren't so easy to recognize in yourself.

The Impostor: acts happy and successful, but is really terrified of failure.
The Rebel: acts like the opinions or good will of others—especially people who are important or powerful—don't matter.
The Loser: acts helpless and unable to cope with the world and waits for someone to come to the rescue.

Does your personality resemble any one of these three?

To improve your self-esteem you must first resist the inner voice that feeds you negative images of yourself. Block out the voices that tell you you're not good enough, smart enough or pretty enough, etcetera. Secondly, you should hold dear your own feelings in an encouraging way in times of difficulty. The way you would uplift others, do the same for yourself. If you've made a mistake, forgive yourself instead of being critical. Thirdly, welcome help from others and openly accept the positive reinforcements they offer you. Isolating yourself and wallowing in self-pity can be dangerous.

Having a good self-image is imperative to having healthy self-esteem. My friend, I'll call Cassie, has the compulsion to constantly catch a glimpse of her appearance in any available reflective surface. For years, we laughed and teased her about annoying us with her habit of constantly checking herself out.

Although an attractive woman with a winning personality, we knew she didn't have this lingering compulsion because she was confident in her looks. On the contrary, she wasn't confident at all in her looks in est., the reason she kept checking out her image from head to toe. We all laughed about it, including Cassie but the seriousness of Body Dysmorphic Disorder—yes, it has a name—is not funny at all.

I asked her what is going on in her head that makes her want to see herself so often. I'm serious when I tell you she catches her reflection in anything: picture windows, glass doors, and any metal surfaces including a freshly washed car. Once she had just started working for a company and when her birthday came her co-workers bought her a full-length mirror for her to keep behind her desk. When she told me, I laughed but told her I couldn't believe that after being there for only a couple of months they had already figured out she couldn't stop looking at herself.

I always knew it was a self-esteem issue I just hadn't run across anything like it. Carol E. Watkins, MD of Healthyspace.com, says BDD is a preoccupation with an imagined physical defect in appearance, or a vastly exaggerated concern about a minimal defect.

For black women, problems like this are ignited and compounded by the images we use to compare our own image against. Starting with television. Cassie is in love with the HBO adult comedy/drama,

Sex in the City. She really loved those white girls, almost like they were her own girlfriends. When the, then Fox network (before moving to UPN) debuted the new sitcom, *Girlfriends* we were all so excited and became instantly hooked. That is, everybody but Cassie. She didn't like it and all she could talk about was Carrie Bradshaw and her three other white counterparts. Boy, did we let her have it. She eventually warmed up to Joan, Lynn, Toni and Maya but not without some constant prodding from her real girlfriends. Sometimes she argues with us and tries to hold her ground but eventually even she has to laugh at herself especially when we ask her if there's a white woman trapped inside of her dying to get out.

When you are constantly seeing images of people who don't look like you it is very damaging to your self-esteem. Or, just as damaging, is continuously seeing negative images of those who *do* look like you. Ladies, please surround yourself with positive images to help you develop a positive identity. Recognizing who you are in Christ and knowing that God created you perfectly and in His image is a great start.

Fear & Forgiveness
Low self-worth broken down is fear manifested. When up against something you believe to be bigger than you, stronger than you or more worthy than you, you feel fear. And fear has many residual effects — anger, helplessness, combativeness, or what I call the "shut down". You either become the

aggressor or you become the victim when feeling or reacting to fear. Either way your worthiness suffers.

When you let go of the spirit of fear and embrace the courageous spirit of love—yes, loving yourself takes courage—then can your self-worth be at its full potential. No man walking this earth is ever at 100% because we are imperfect. That is, our bodies are mortal, therefore imperfect but our souls are perfect. Our perfect souls are residing inside our flawed flesh and because of this we have forgotten or don't realize that through the ultimate Spirit we are perfect. According to Hebrews 10:14, God made us perfect because of the sacrifice and crucifixion of Christ. As long as we are alive on earth and walking in flesh, we are imperfect.

When you have low self worth you either become the snake or the turtle. You strike out at others or you retreat. People who often sit silently by when they should speak up, often will speak up at inappropriate times and those who are constantly ranting and raving won't take a stand at the very moment when they should.

Self-improvement

Gossip is a thief. I'm not talking about what I've seen others do, I'm talking about what I, myself have done. When I used to sit around gossiping about others I lost time I could've used for introspection, raising my consciousness, serving others or developing other elements of self-growth.

Forwarding email messages about Usher and Tameka — people who have no idea I even exist — was a time and growth stealer. Not just lost time — this is precious enough — but lost energy.

I also believe whenever we do things like gossip, lie or any other negative thing we do that is a time stealer, the ugly energy put out in the atmosphere is lingering around waiting to re-attach itself to us.

When you really want to make a change you have to start doing things differently. Start with the small things but don't stop there. Let it evolve into bigger things and when your actions change so will your thoughts.

Self-improvement may take years — in fact it's a life-long journey. The saying, "Act the way you want to be, and soon you'll be the way you act" works. Start by doing something as simple as not engaging in conversations of lower instincts, meaning useless banter that adds no value to anyone's quality of life. It will soon lessen your desire for other time stealing activities.

When you sit around talking about what others are doing or shouldn't be doing instead of doing what you should be doing then moments and good energy that should be yours has lost the opportunity to be yours. You've missed out. And you alone hold the power to elevate your quality of life.

X-ing negative people out of your life

I don't like to attend funerals. Let me rephrase that. I REALLY don't like to attend funerals. If I go to one it's because I really cared for the deceased or family members of the deceased. You just won't find me out there going to the funeral of everyone that I know who has passed on. This may seem a little unorthodox but I've learned to use this as a gauge on whether or not to continue to interact personally with someone. I ask myself would I attend their funeral should they pass away? If I wouldn't give you my time in death (not to say I wouldn't still mourn the loss) why would I give you precious moments of my time in life.

This may seem heartless but I don't mean it to be. Time is one of the most valued gifts we have and we should be wise about how we spend it. Learn how to gracefully X people out of your life who are holding you back from your purpose or set poor examples of the greatness you want in your life.

Toxic people are not always easy to identify at first, but eventually you it becomes apparent. Have you ever known someone that after you leave them you feel like the life has been sucked out of you? You always feel bad after you have spent time with them. This may be a co-worker, a family member or a close friend. It is never easy to rid yourself of such people mostly because by the time you realize how toxic they are you don't know how to divorce yourself from the relationship. Part of the toxicity is the role in which you played in being there to take in the poison. This dance doesn't work unless it has two partners.

The first step you take in ridding yourself of a toxic person in your life is to make the decision to do so. After that, you will know just how to distance yourself from that person in a way that will work. You can flat-out tell them of your decision, stop answering their calls, refrain from going to gatherings where you will run into them.

Good Hair/Bad Hair, Weight Gain and Other Negative Images

My clients from back during the height of my career were well versed in the fact that there were certain terms I didn't allow in my salon. It was always funny how when some new, unsuspecting client would wander in and use the phrase "good hair" how everyone would sing a chorus of "oooo" knowing that I would soon be coming unglued.

The term, "good hair", was describing hair, which closely resembles European hair, and "bad hair" meaning any hair more like African hair. This language may not be used as much as it used to be but the residual affects of slavery are still so very much alive. This is another way of keeping our self-esteem stagnant and lacking. And it works both ways.

We know we eat the wrong things, as well as too much of the wrong things, yet we continue when we are privy to information on better nutrition and healthy foods.

Black women have been looked down upon by each other for wearing their hair straight as well as wearing their hair natural. When is the self-loathing going to end? That's right—self-loathing when we attack each other we are attacking ourselves. When we speak poorly of others we think poorly of ourselves. Why, after so many years are we still using our White counterparts as guides by whom we measure practically everything?

It's no secret that black women are some of the most full-figured women on the planet; and this is something we've had little problem accepting—in fact, we brag on it. But, there is a difference between embracing our curves, and neglecting our health. Not taking care of our bodies is another way of devaluing ourselves. Over-eating or emotional eating, a lack of exercise, and neglecting health problems are ways in which black women fail themselves.

Plain and simple, we live in a time where information is at our fingertips. We know we eat the wrong things, as well as too much of the wrong things, yet we continue when we are privy to information on better nutrition and healthy foods. What is that about?

We know that we work too hard, are overly stressed and don't get enough exercise, but we continue on while watching our mothers and grandmothers have 'poor-diet' related illnesses (strokes, heart attacks, heart disease, diabetes, and the like). We know better, but we don't do better. We fry every piece of meat we prepare, pile cheese and ranch dressing on everything we eat (either that or gravy). We don't drink water, we cook all of the nutrients out of our vegetables and God forbid we consider fruit when it's snack time.

I understand how hard making the change is, believe me. If I had to trade in butter for margarine (what is margarine anyway?) I'd probably go on a hunger strike. The answer is, everything in moderation.

When you're preparing Sunday dinner, don't have ham *and* pork chops, then put a piece of salt pork in your greens or green beans, then drown your mashed potatoes, corn on the cob and dinner rolls in butter. This sounds very similar to meals I've cooked in the past. We can eat some of these things some of the time, but the problem is eating it all of the time.

It's really simple:

- Drink plenty of water
- Do not over cook your vegetables
- Eat more fruit
- Consider methods other than frying when cooking your meats
- Cut down on your portions
- Choose healthy snacks

After working hard all day, and then coming home to do more work, we feel like we don't need to do any more moving about because we've been on the go all day. But, exercise is good for more than just moving the body about, and breaking a sweat. It clears your mind, relieves stress, and helps you to find inner peace.

More on ridding stress from out lives.

Final Questions:

1. What are your feelings on women who date or marry men based on how much money they have?
2. Do you believe yourself to have healthy views on sex and sexuality?
3. What is your own personal truth on unmarried sex?
4. If you never marry will you be comfortable taking a vow of celibacy?
5. Do you believe that marriage is God's purpose for you?
6. Have you realistically considered the fact that you may never marry? What are your feelings on this?
7. Is low self-esteem an issue for you and are you willing to do something about it?
8. Are there areas in your personal health that you need to make changes? Diet, exercise, or see your doctor?

Summation of Sections:

Marriage is a calling

Don't assume, because you have romantic notions and feelings that being married is your calling or purpose in life. Know what it is you're wishing for and know when God is standing in agreement with you on the decisions you make.

What are your examples of marriages?

If marriage is your calling, understand the examples you've witnessed in your life of other married couples and even the single people who have helped to frame your views on love and holy matrimony.

Marriage is for the Grown & Sexy

Be honest with yourself. Are you really mature enough to handle being married? Once real maturity steps in you will be wise enough to make a decision on whether you truly want to even involve yourself in an espousal union.

The Divorce from Hell

Be perceptive of the men you spend your time with. There are always signs in the beginning, they're just so easy to overlook when your eyes are full of stars and your body is consumed with the tingles.

Single, saved, and sexually satisfied

Find your own personal truth. Be wise, intelligent, and know who you are. Handle your business and take care of yourself, mind, body and soul.

Final Thought; *Will having the benefits of marriage be worth the work you have to put in? Only you can answer this question for yourself.*

If you believe marriage is your calling, this book may have indirect advice for you but for clear-cut information on being successfully married, or preparing yourself for marriage, I recommend the following books:

The Act of Marriage: The Beauty of Sexual Love, by Tim & Beverly La Haye

Dating the Divorced Man, by Christie Hartman PH.D
Fatherless Daughters, by Pamela Thomas

The Five Love Languages, by Gary Chapman

Lies at the Alter: The Truth About Great Marriages, Dr. Robin L. Smith

The Proper Care & Feeding of Marriage, Dr. Laura Schlessinger

101 Things I Wish I Knew When I Got Married, Linda & Charles Bloom

Reference:

Section 1:

1. Rick Warren, The Purpose Driven Life (Michigan, Zondervan 2002), 27.

Section 2:

2. Gary Smalley, *For Better Or For Best: Understand Your Man* (New York Harper Collins Publishers 1979, 1982, 1988), 35.
3. United States Census Bureau, http://www.census.gov/population/cen2000/phc-t11/tab01.pdf
4. Dr. Jill Waggoner, *My Sister's Keeper: Is Your Temple In Order?* (Dallas, My Sister's Keeper Press 2004), 96.
5. William Shakespeare, *Hamlet*

Section 3:

6. Sheron C. Patterson, *Put On Your Crown: The lack Woman's Guide to Living Single (... and Christian)* (Ohio, Pilgrim Press 2006), 64.
7. Kathy Freston, The One: *The One: Finding Soul Mate Love And Making It Last* (New York, Hyperion 2006), 16.
8. Big Boom, If You Want Closure in Your Relationship, Start with Your Legs (New York Simon & Schuster 2007), 11.

Section 4:

9. Gary Chapman, *The Five Love Languages* (Chicago, Northfield Publishing 1995), 36.
10. Daniel Whyte III, Letters To Young Black Men: Advice and Encouragement for a Difficult Journey (Torch Legacy Publications, Dallas/Atlanta 2005), 103.
11. CBS, http://www.cbsnews.com/stories/2007/04/12/nri onL/Min2675273_Pfw1.ahrml

Section 5:

12. Tim & Beverly LaHaye, *The Act of Marriage: The Beauty of Sexual Love* (Grand Rapids, Zondervan 1976, 1998), 71.
13. David Zinczenko, *Men, Love & Sex: Then Complete User's Guide for Women* (New York, Rodale 2006), 113.
14. Carol E. Watkins, MD, http://www.healthyplace.com/Communities/Anx iety/body_dysmorphic_disorder.asp, (2001)

Books by Elaine Flowers

Black Beauty

It's Morning; Torn Lovers and Their Stories

Broken Appointments

8137471R0